Nova Scotia:

Nova Scotia: **Window on the Sea**

Nova Scotia:
Window
on the Sea

Text by Ernest Buckler
Photographs by Hans Weber

Clarkson N. Potter, Inc./Publisher   NEW YORK
DISTRIBUTED BY CROWN PUBLISHERS, INC.

Library of Congress Catalog Card
Number: 73-75378

ISBN: 0-517-50382-4

Published simultaneously in Canada
by McClelland and Stewart Limited

Inquiries should be addressed to
Clarkson N. Potter, Inc.,
419 Park Avenue South,
New York, N.Y. 10016

First edition

Design: David Shaw

Printed in Canada

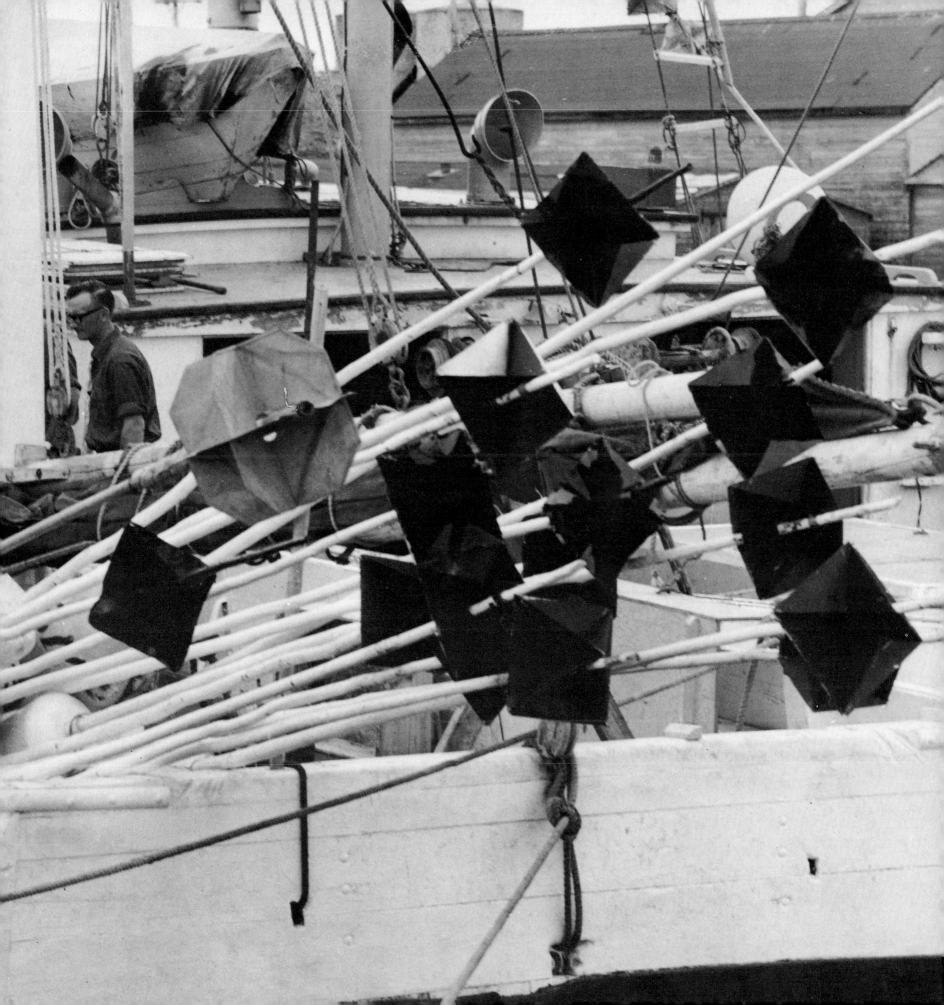

Contents

Amethysts and Dragonflies

Nova Scotia is nearly an island, nearly the last place left where place and people are not thinned and adulterated with graftings that grow across the grain. Yet what saves it from insularity is a peninsularity like that of the heart. The arteries go out to the Main, but the beat is all of itself.

Sometimes it seems self-contradictory. It is grounded in the sea, but rooted in the land. Its features are as varied as those of the body.

As the hand is entirely different from the eye, so is the ripple of breeze, weighted with light, that shot-silks the strawberried grass in the peace-rivered Gaspereau different from the hippopotamus rocks the elemental sea fumes against in a thunderstorm at Peggy's Cove.

As the throat is entirely different from the lung, so is the everlasting shudder of Time in Port Royal (where North America started) different from the Now-light in the eyes of children swimming in the meadow brook when the last load of hay they've raked after has been landed in the sweltering barn.

Yet as the body is "one", for all its variousness, so is Nova Scotia. Its capes, coves, lochs, bays and harbours jigsaw its coastline as if whoever was its architect had let his pencil stray without direction. Yet it remains a whole.

Its mountains take on no Cabot lordliness. They chat like uncles with their nephew valleys. Even the rocks have no stoniness. Houses (though their eyes may be as different as brothers' from cousins' or great-aunts') agree with each other, noddingly, and swap kinship the day long.

In its cities or near-cities (other than Halifax, where the myth-softened mask of a history which has been unique as nowhere else pervades even the impervious) pavements, as in cities everywhere, beat the faces blind. But elsewhere people keep their hearts on the latch.

Men at Grand Pré, tired to blurring, knock clods of earth off the ploughshare that has turned the last restorative furrow in the clover field and, long after Evangeline, west their feet homeward to suppertime and what is still the spirit of lantern light.

Men, blurred by faith (though not scared of the sacred) light candles in the great cathedral at Church Point which overawes the patient waterside like Christ Galilee.

Men at Sober Island sink nets into the sombre sea and draw up its deep (the mackerel gasping like thought with its mouth open) hand over rope-storied hand.

Men at Beaver River shock the living slumber out of giant maples with their gleaming axe blades before they fell them in a sweep majestic as the fall of empires, their muscles sterner than bone in the frozen day.

Men in Cape Breton go down into the dark of the earth for the wood of eons made coal....

But they are all the same kind of man.

Sober Island. Wine Harbour. Folly Lake. Bible Brook.... Some of the place names sound quaint. But the people are not.

They are no quainter than trees. Their faces may be gnarled as knuckles. They may be wrenched from any formal beauty by the erosion of dailiness. But they are not shuttered by the city wariness, not scoundreled by the lie of openness assumed, not mineralized by the poison pellet at the core of all tyrannical ambition. Their eyes see through sham at a glance; but they are not themselves contagioned by it or squinted or gimleted.

Some people are dilettantes of themselves. Nova Scotians people ply their own verb for all it's worth. Each is himself because he does not imitate — any more than a tree tries to turn itself into a geranium.

In the great cities, man is forever lonely because he never sees his thoughts and feelings corporified outside him, so that the crush of their edgelessness is lessened. In Nova Scotia, no man but can see (whether he sees what he sees or not) the shape of his thoughts and feelings in print, so to speak, almost everywhere he looks or hears:

The elixir of winning in the sound of the pine trees making their own breeze.

The gusts of longing for someone gone that bend the heart so low no sigh can do anything to exhale them, in the stretching fields that shimmer the greener for the very nowhereness in them of the one who was once your everywhere.

The gull-shaped thought in the thought-shaped gull.

The sheen of health in the bluejay's wing.

The pang of age first seen as the one thing that never stops for a moment's recess, in the calendered beech leaves.

The bound of joy, in the sound of the sun-up nails being driven into the concurring boards in the house the man is building for his family in sight of the tidal river.

The dinginess (yes, that too) of those days when the windows in the lighthouse of the mind are streaked with the grime of failed hopes, when you feel you are neglectable in the eyes of others (as in your own you are no more than a neglectable question), when everything is now diminished to itself divided by a thousand —there it is in the scrawny featherless necks of the four fledgling sparrows huddled dead in the rain-soaked nest.

The tawdriness of the mind's sullen moment picking its teeth—there it is in the Javex can made into a windmill at the end of the unweeded driveway where it meets the asphalt . . . .

But never farther off than the unspoken can reach is the surety that gives a man his cadence: in the stormproof forests and the everlasting sea.

Nowhere flawlessly beautiful, Nova Scotia is often for that very reason the more beautiful, as one face is sometimes lovelier to another for its very plainnesses.

Neither stately nor mansioned in any one quality, it has yet a watermark all its own which it stamps (invisibly but no less distinguishably) on each of its particulars. Though they are as multiform as the bibliography of seed.

It is amethysts in the imperial rocks at Blomidon, and snow apples in the consentful orchards of the Valley.

It is a black bear in the blueberry barrens, and the sun afternooning on the village grave of a child aged six.

It is the train blowing lonesome as Lincoln's at all the crossings from Yarmouth to Hawkesbury, and the leap of the confettied trout in the stream that feeds the sawmill where the fresh-cut shingles smell clean as morning.

It is the grey December blizzard, hard-hearted as sleeplessness, that unites everything it scourges, from the careworn house on the speechless hill to the house proud of the street it's on . . . and the April breeze, its penitence, that awakens the seed to its future.

It is the oxen of the muscle and the cavalry (or the Calvary) of the senses.

It is picks and shovels and canoes (which, another way, spell "oceans") and shotguns (which, another way, misspell "snug").

It is the terrible silences in the breast of the man whose wage permits his family little more than bread, and the thunderclap of rum and harmonicas.

It is silver birches (and their shadows) in the silver moonlight.

It is the sun coming up like an anthem behind the daily hills, and the sun descending into the haunts of yesterday where those moments charged with the light and conclusions of life are so deathlessly kept . . . .

Here, each man has seen the pear blossom, all perfection, and smelled the wild roses on the stone wall.

He has felt the heart's rejoicing and the heart's face fall.

He has held, long and hard, those things that the arms or the eyes can hold (the flesh, the present images), and he has gazed, heart-staggered, at the flesh not there, at the touch refused. At the information of what the arms or the eyes can never quite reach:

The dragonfly rising from the landlocked brook, its wings a shimmer as they hold it absolutely still, to make its statement on the boundless air.

   The wild geese flying arrowed, their statement with them, into the indecipherable clouds.

   The hush of meaning that the train whistle dying out has made form of....

He has seen the *natural*, with its grace never learned, but never insecure like learning's:

   The sap (by its own command) rising in the sugar maple.

   The apple (by its own map) shaping itself on the bough.

   The daisy forming its own petals as no human conjurer could.

   The earth itself living out what it was born with, totally without artifice....

Nova Scotia is the face from Genesis and the face from Ruth. The face from Greco and the face from Rubens. The life from Faulkner and the life from Hardy....

   It is a dictionary where the seasons look up their own meanings and test them. It is a sea-son where men can man their own helms.

Masts and Anchors

More than the land, the sea is a metaphor for everything. And more than anywhere else, in Nova Scotia.

Bronzed with calm in that special twilight when things look at themselves after a sunstruck day, with waves no larger than the smallest of sighs as they rock each other and the anchored dory gentler than kisses, it is blows forgiven.

When it petticoats the beaches with ruffles of foam, it is a theorem of docility and goodwill.

When, savage with loneliness, it sends its waves gliding like frenzied whales to a roaring peak three times the height of a man, then down again to the valleys beneath them that are not like valleys at all but cauldrons of fury (while the sun, which has already doomsdayed the earth with the outcast light that has no light behind it, and set free the mindless howling that lurks behind the Sunday face of wind or snow or rain, darkens it the colour of omens), it is the cannons of unreason which besiege the temples of the mind.

Fuming at the slightest intervention, fuming at the rocks that are all gravity and never change, it is the anarchy of a jealoused blood . . . .

But the Nova Scotians who live by the sea that is their living do not toy with metaphors or the toys of words. They don't weigh their words, for words weigh less than smoke on the scales they count the solid pounds of the day's catch with. Not poets (except as there may be poetry in the hands of men who take their lives in their hands daily), for them only the real is real. A mast is a mast. A hull is a hull. An oar is an oar.

Their muscles are not the athlete's plaything muscles, but the sinews of endurance. Their merchandise is not the shop-made gewgaws that pass across the city counters, but the stuff of life.

Waking at the brisk of dawn, they draw on their clothing soberly, as men do who face a day with their task's name on it.

Daybreak bisects the sea with a stripe of golden coins, as if Moses had struck a glittering path across it. But they know there is no path. Stronger than drowning (though they never know this, nor ever reflect that the man who is equal to the sea is the equal of everything), they dare its yawning tracklessness as men brave doubt.

Snug in their kitchened house where the kettle says "wife" and the scribbler says "child", the sea is the everlasting There. But when they are on it, it is the absolute Here, and the house is a continent of Thereness away.

The sea is forever lonely. Its only company is the moon. Nothing grows on it. No trees, the land's spokesmen. No grass, the land's peacemaker. No flowers, the land's song. Only (beneath it) the nerveless fish that are all nervousness and those unlikeliest of creatures, the ones within shells. None of them able to make a sound, not even the silent hum that the land's growth makes.

The sea is unfeeling and implacable. No one has ever broken its code. Yet it says more to the men who work on it with their iron-boned grace than anything else.

The wives keep such a fearful eye on it that it seems almost to be brought inside them as a feature of their consciousness. Yet they do not curse it as one curses something false. Even the ghosts of the drowned have a quality of sincerity and deathlessness about them that no others of the dead do.

Young Nova Scotians bestride the sea. Yet it salts their blood with a kind of wistfulness. (Where exactly is the where of all things?)

And when a man becomes too old to climb a mast or cast an anchor, he weaves nets as intricate as the shawl of an Infanta.

And when he becomes too old for that as well, the sea is so imperishably in him that sitting sunning in the lee of it, he builds a ship inside a bottle. While he dreams of his long voyage once to India or of the trip he never made around the Horn.

Man and Snowman

If the sea infixes some nameless and unslakeable yearning in a man's eyes, the farm yokes the facts of memory to his every breath. And more than the fisherman with his single-hearted gaze, he comes to be the sum, substance and museum of its thronging assembly.

A farmer, age upon him, lies on his bed at Bras d'Or. (Or it could be Christmas Island or Sheet Harbour.) His body, twin of him, has betrayed him.

The strange thing, there had never been any pain. Not even at the start. Just that painless blow somewhere inside his head as he lifted the wig of hay from the rack, so heavy the fork buckled with it. It was like a hammer blow of sound, and then his left side going dead like a sound gone.

He couldn't remember being carried from the barn. But when he came to in his bedroom his mind was as clear as it had ever been. He could see. He could hear. But he couldn't move his head, or walk alone — or speak.

They put a slate beside his good hand. (An old one of his own he thought it must be, for children had not used slates these many years.) On it he could write down any questions he had, or tell them of any needs.

He hadn't written a word since he left school: at fourteen, because his own aging father had needed his stout muscle on the farm. The slate pencil, his most likely too, felt clumsy in his fingers. But he could make himself understood.

The family (his son and his son's wife and the grandchildren, Mark and Paul) felt none of that burdensome recoil so often touched off by sickness in the old. They tended him as involvedly as if he was nineteen.

At first they'd come into his bedroom every evening and tell him all that had happened that day. What they'd done. The people they'd seen. What they'd heard and what they thought about it. Down to the last detail.

But gradually, a proud man, he came to discourage this demand on them.

Gradually, not to bother them, he ceased to write any questions on the slate. Now, all he wrote was "yes" or "no".

"Are you all right?"

"Yes."

"Do you want anything?"

"No."

Sometimes he wanted death. Anything to free him from the silence the walls ticked with and the pattern of purple ivy that stamped itself so tirelessly on the wallpaper. But he never wrote anything like that.

They never neglected him. They never left him alone in the house. And tied to his spool bed, on the rung nearest his good hand, was a bell he could ring if he had to get out onto the "chair". A tinkler off the string of sleighbells he had himself sewn to the leather thongs the day he drove Ellen in to town to marry her.

He minded the chair as nothing in his life before. Even when the son came. When the wife came it was agony. And once while she was bathing him and at the pressure of the warm cloth he came alive down there he had never felt so bitterly reduced.

They switched his bed around so that his head faced the window. So that he could see nearly all the fields and the movements in them, and the pasture that ran back to the steep spruce mountain.

He watched them sow the seeds in the land he'd been the first to break. He watched them hay where he had sown the first clover. The silence ceased to tick then.

But he couldn't see the path that led to the meadow. He couldn't see the grove of saplings where the son used to play under his eye while he cut the hoop poles. And sometimes, when a movement would vanish beyond the edges of the rectangle of fields the window framed, he would feel like tearing the walls apart.

But his back was in no way broken. He was the man who can bear more than he can bear.

All this last week he'd watched the grandchildren and their friends building snow forts in the field just outside the window. Mounding them to the height their arms could reach, scraping the edges smooth with a barrel stave, then playing Blindman's Buff amongst them the way he'd played it once amongst the cocks of August hay.

Today he watched them make a snowman. The air was soft as silk. The great globes of snow they rolled up to form the body left tracks right down to the aftergrass that was still green. They patted the small globe of the head into shape until it was perfectly round.

There were two black coals for its eyes, one for its nose, and smaller ones for its teeth. They put a pipe he knew was his between its teeth. (How many times he'd tapped the stem of that pipe against his own teeth as he sat by the well curb in the Sunday sun and talked the week's work over with a neighbour!) And on its head they placed an old slouch hat that he saw was his too.

There was a game he had come to play with his memory. Off and on since he'd first heard Paul, the grandson who was named for him, counting 5, 10, 15, 20 . . . while the others ran to hide.

A bitter thought had skimmed his mind. What blindfold God was forever counting 5, 10, 15, 20 . . .? And where did you hide when the count was 65, 70? Years. But his mind had always "thrown" a bitter thought, the way a fish throws the hook. It did then.

And then it simply seemed to him that, yes, the years of his life had been grouped into just such sections. That if his mind could just piece these sections together again, like building blocks . . . .

In the kitchen, the son's wife said: "Did you tell him Karl was asking about him? He missed Karl so when the family moved to town."

"No," the son said. "I forgot. And . . . I don't know. There's no way to be sure. But do you think he always takes things in?"

"I don't know," she said. Her knitting needles turned the heel of a sock. "How *was* Karl? Is he well?"

"I guess so," he said. "But every time I go to town I see him sitting there in that same place. That bench beside the Post Office. Just sitting there moving the tip of his cane back and forth over the sidewalk. He looks like an old, old man."

"It's funny, isn't it," she said. "*He* still looks so young, doesn't he."

5, 10.

He'd thought this block would be out of reach. So long ago. But when he closed his eyes it came back clearer than yesterday. It was as if he held it right there in his hand and could turn it from one windowed side to another.

It was running . . . and bread . . . and wool . . . and sleep . . . and moss . . . and minnows . . . and breezes . . . and bobsleds . . . and rock tops . . . and tree forks . . . and dreams of thrones (seen on the coloured pages of the Bible with pictures in it) . . . and mornings (each one with prizes and surprises in it) . . . and hills . . . and hollows . . . and sunburn . . . and somersaults . . . and hours and hours and hours and hours . . . .

And, yes, right at the centre was that one day, that one teeming June day when everything seemed to be so sparklingly in place.

He'd been walking behind his father in the path of the plough. At the bottom of the third furrow his father said: "Would you like to ride on the horse's back for a few turns?"

There was a moment's fear, but he said yes.

His father lifted him up and told him to hang tight to the hames. The hames, each with a gleaming brass knob on the end of it, curved upward like the twin arms of a lyre.

They started off again, and all at once it was as if his heart let loose a cage of swifts. He felt so high above the earth that he could touch where the sky began. The roll of the horse's muscles seemed like a mightiness of his own, the roll of the turning sod like a song.

He knew that the horse would keep straight to the furrow with no guidance at all, but he gripped the hames, veering them a little this way or that, as if through them he was steering the whole world. And always would....

Downstairs, the wife said: "Mark, go up and see if your grandfather wants anything."

"All right," Mark said. "But he never does."

...15, 20....

That block was easy too. Not as easy as the one before: here and there it was clouded (because it had been clouded then) by such a blizzard of feelings discovered for the first time. But he could remember it all if he tried.

It was striding. It was flesh. It was health in you like a brimming yes. It was never a thought of taking your time about anything, never a thought of caution, never looking back over your shoulder. It was the weight of things giving way to the strength (bottomless muscles of it) to lift them. It was straight ahead, but it wasn't scurry. It was news, always new, coming from everything you looked at. It was taking all the jumps, bare-hearted, in the solid stirrups of your blood....

Sometimes it was the bright scarlet brawl of temper. Once he'd smashed the peavey stock to bits against a rock because a split in it had pinched his hands that were so quick to anger.

And once there was terror.

One afternoon he and Karl and Leo, who were always together, decided to swim the lake at its widest, the naked three of them. Sun and water sang against

53

their nakedness: it was naked glee.

But when they were half-way across, the sun went in and the water looked like night water. He wished he could put his feet down, touching bottom, and walk ashore. He began to swim as if it was running after dark. He swam until the far shore looked so near he was sure that now he must be in the shallows next the bank.

Forgetting how distance over water could fool you, he let his feet down and his head went under. In the moment before he flailed himself back to the surface he was seized with naked fear. For the first time in his life he had a glimpse of how the calmest second could suddenly open wide and show the terrible jaws lurking behind it.

But in less than five minutes more he *was* in the shallows, then climbing up the bank.

The sun came out of the cloud and, as he rested on the bank beside Karl and Leo, with the three of them such sun-brothers that each was made three times himself, even the memory of his fear was swallowed up without a trace.

That's how it was then. It was knowing that, no matter what deep water you got into, the bank was always there.

It was striding. It was a dreaming so much thinner-skinned than the child's spectator dreaming that he was vividly right there inside it. And after the first so altogether different dream he'd had about a girl, it was the strut at the very centre of him. As if he carried in that sweet liquor of himself the power and thrust of all creation.

In the kitchen the wife said: "Did you tell him Leo was dead?"

"No," the son said. "I didn't know what to do. I didn't want to upset him. Do you think he'd remember Leo, anyway?"

54

"I think he might," she said. "Yesterday when I took the broth up to him I told him I'd made it from the two partridge you'd shot for him in that wild apple tree at the edge of the burntland. I think he understood."

"And do you remember way back at the first?" he said. "When he kept writing 'deed' on the slate and we thought it was 'dead' and he was wandering? Until Paul —wasn't it?—guessed that what he wanted was to make the place over to me while he could still sign?"

"Yes." She smiled. "It's funny about the children," she said. "Most children shy away from anyone sick. But Paul and Mark . . . if they've made something in school . . . or anything . . . the first thing they get into the house they run up to show him. Before they even take their coats off. I never have to ask them to."

"Kids always liked him," the son said. "And it was strange, because he never made that much fuss over them. He was always just so . . . well, steady. He never let bad luck—or bad news—or anything else—get the best of him." His eyes went suddenly still. "I only ever seen him cry but the once. It was one day he didn't have the money to take me to the circus in town." His eyes came back as breath does after a sigh. "Do you think I should tell him about Leo, then?"

"I would."

"All right," the son said. "I'll tell him in the morning."

. . . 25 . . . .

That was the city block.

For a moment a greyness the shade of the brain's own grey shadowed his mind as it does when you recall some step in your life so mistaken that it seems to have been the act of a total stranger. Another moment and the dimness vanished in the light of the memory's sheer chiseling force.

At first the thought of working in the city, if only at a flagman's job with a construction crew, was all excitement. The wheels of the train taking him there had seemed like a steed of adventure he was riding. It overrode even the imprint of Ellen's face (fixed in its last look as the faces of people you leave are, and stationary as italics) at the station.

But after a week of nights in the rented room, a sense of suffocation grew.

The room's walls seemed to wall in all the scuffed fallout of the shabby dreams (or had there been any at all?) of the men (their lives rented, too, as cheaply as possible) who had stared at this ceiling before him. He began to feel as if the tale of his own life was not in ink of any kind but in chalk.

The months went by like blinded oxen. This feeling of emptiness went deeper and deeper.

Here, in the city, it was as if, though nothing ever stood still, nothing moved. He had never taken orders (except from the sun). Here, he had to take orders, without question, from a man whose back he could have broken with one hammerlock of his plough-hardened muscles.

And every day the innumerable blows on his huddled homesick heart. From the scabrous state that city things (like drunks) fall into. Or from the oblivious:

Scum-sloshed pilings in the bilgewater of the harbour.

Tram cars, bound to their tracks, climbing the hilly streets, with all their occupants so glazed with monotony that none of them notices how streets can choke the life-reach out of hills even.

Sirens screaming fire; and other (silent) sirens screaming accidents to the spirit, itself too dulled to know the grazing wound from the fatal.

Water besmirching itself in the gutter where the sodden poster lies.

Clouds beclouding themselves with puzzlement at the scrambled alphabet below.

Labels, labels, labels, everywhere . . . loudmouthing the trivial contents they enwrap.

No singing birds.

No gladness in the fountain in the Mall.

No two things, however close, less than the distance of effigies apart. Neither the bottle caps and the slush beneath the rusted sign with the capitals missing. Nor the amusements like the gargoyles of fun, and the endless Sundays when the blind factory windows (and the prison eyes in the locked-up shops) out-hollow the hollow church bells until it becomes as when not even the letters of your own name stir any response in you.

The trees in the park so captive and denatured that they impose a gloss of loneliness even lonesomer than the sleepwalking movements of the men and women indoored at the same worthless tasks day in and day out.

The crumpled bill that is the only link between the merchant and his customer.

The telephone poles that bear the wires overhead, that are as deaf as money to the messages they bear; as deaf as the object longing seeks to the cries within the messages that swarm through them....

And in the street:

The boss-faced men, and the clock-stopped faces of the others.

The faces that look like an article of clothing bought uncertainly and never worn thereafter with satisfaction.

The faces that look as if they had been slept (or nightmared) in.

Men's hands womanized by pen and paper.

The eyes that neither give nor lend nor borrow.

The mouths like a "fault" in cement, looking as if they were clamped tight on their own curb bits....

Sometimes the city like some monstrous dragon in a child's dream of dragons he'd seen on a page, the soot of exile fuming from its nostrils. Sometimes like a giant shell-backed insect on its back, its million legs flailing helplessly in the air....

Until one day near the end of this first crippling year there he caught a glimpse in the street of a girl's face so like Ellen's, so (with all the grit that plunders the flesh left out) like a vision of Ellen's, that he was staggered.

That afternoon when the foreman shouted at him, "Get a move on there! What the hell do you think you're doin', havin' your picture taken?", he gave him his fist in the greatest hallelujah it had ever felt.

That night he took the midnight train home.

. . . 25, 30, 35, 40, 45, 50 . . . .
A single pattern made these blocks as one.

It was eating with Ellen, sleeping with Ellen, working with Ellen, laughing with Ellen, having Ellen to turn to . . . .

It was being each other's total hearer and hearth.

It was having every threat a safety away from striking him on any naked nerve, because loving Ellen was the nerve of him that cushioned all the rest from the last thing that nerves can not withstand: forlornness.

(It was a little like being freedomly stormstayed inside a warm cordial house that has the spirit of mulled wine.)

Smoke rising, dew falling, wheels turning, sun, rain, snow . . . with Ellen there, it was having all the good things in the year's teeming calendar as near to him as the touch of his own blood and all the stony ones a flint-proof skin apart.

It was day after day of wholeness without a sliver of hankering to enpustule it.

It was putting his own son on the horse's back when he ploughed.

It was the daily bread of hope not bred in doubt — but more than hope, it was home.

Ellen . . . Ellen . . . Ellen . . . . Her name flaked down through his mind as gently as the snowflakes eddied down outside the window, and he slept. He slept, and he dreamed.

He dreamed about the night Ellen died, the year he was 50.

He saw the burning sunset paint the colours of pain he'd never felt the likes of, on the blind church windows. He felt the beating his heart took from the skulls of everything he looked at that her hands would never touch again or her eyes ever see. Each leaf, each stone, each blade of grass, had printed on it, each in its own alphabet, the one word "gone" — each of them itself as if gone out of reach. He saw the gaping socket of unrelatedness inside him, now that she was forever out of sight....

He awoke, nearly choked with the sound of crying his throat couldn't make.

Downstairs, the wife was hearing young Paul's spellings.

"Trance . . . Tranquil . . . Transient...."

"What does 'transient' mean?" Paul asked.

She didn't know. She looked at her husband.

"I don't know, either," he said. "Go find it in that big dictionary of your grand-father's." He looked at the sunset that was all bruise and flame. "You know," he said slowly, "he hardly went to school much, but he was always reading. Anything he could get hold of. He knew what all kinds of long words meant. If he'd been born somewhere else...."

"I'm not so sure," the wife said. "You could never get him to talk about that time he spent in the city, could you."

"He slept a lot today," she added. "I think he's failing."

"Maybe . . . a little," the son said. "But he always had that strong constitution."

"What does 'constitution' mean?" Paul asked.

The dream slipped away to wherever dreams go, taking its freight of feeling with it. His mind went back to his game. Or was it a task now? There was a new sense of urgency about it. A sudden drive to have it over with.

. . . 55, 60, 65. . . .

Yes, yes, those blocks too were fairly clear. Clear enough, anyway, that in this new haste to reach the end he could skip them, come back to them later. Fill them in later, once the capstone block of 70 was, all conquered, fitted into place.

For they were lasting, simply. Finding out that if you put the sickened heart to work again, and soon, a different set of scopes and muscles grew. Finding that whatever life might rob you of, you were always left with *something* worth its cost. Learning that. . . .

But surely all you had learned, any answers there might be, would be contained in that last block.

He skipped to 70.

"I left his window up a crack this afternoon," the wife said, "to air the room out. Paul, would you go up and put it down? It looks like rain. But don't disturb him."

. . . 70 . . . 70 . . . 70. . . .

His mind wrestled with it. But in a kind of dismay he found he couldn't force it into the shape of anything whatsoever.

He was completely blocked. Why, why, he asked himself, could he call up those early years so easily and yet be helpless to picture the day he was 70? A day that was hardly a month ago, he was sure.

Again and again he tried. But each time, his mind caught itself, before he knew it, slewing backward. 60, 60, 60 . . . so many measures! 60 seconds in a minute . . . 60 minutes in an hour . . . 60 pounds in a bushel of potatoes . . . 60 degrees (and where was his carpenter's protractor now?) in each angle of a rafter wedge that had all sides the same. . . .

Again and again he reined his mind back to its object, trying to storm the image of his seventieth birthday clear. But again and again he met only a wall blanker than smoke, a nowhere louder than silence, a stare whiter than zeroes. Again . . . and again . . . and again . . . .

Until, quite suddenly, as when you step into the star-cooled clearing after a day with the axe in the knotted thicket of rock hemlock that you hadn't given up on until it was all felled and limbed and piled . . . as then, a wash of total serenity went through and through him.

He didn't touch the bell. But he reached for the slate pencil in the dark.

The rain started softly, as if it was picking its steps; then poured in earnest all night long.

The snow forts were dissolved, and the snowman melted gradually until there was nothing left of it but the coals and the pipe and the hat, drenched dark, but with the darker sweat stains on the band still showing.

In the morning, when the son went into the bedroom and found his father dead, there was one word scrawled on the slate. None of them could puzzle it out for certain.

The wife thought it was "please". The son, "praise". Mark thought it was "price".

"No, no," Paul said, "it's 'peace'."

"How old was he?" the woman who wrote up deaths for the town newspaper asked.

"Not quite seventy," the wife said. "Not till this coming Friday. The date's right there in the Bible."

"He always had a strong constitution, didn't he," Paul said, nearly crying but proud of this word he'd learned.

"Yes," the father said. "He had his good times and his bad times . . . but if anyone ever had the stuff in him . . . or got the most out of life . . . *he* did."

Faces and Universes

To speak of Nova Scotia is not to speak of its thoroughfares of traffic, business, learning.... These are the same here as everywhere: where the din of striving and the tin of words deface the face and put the price tags on it. The heart of this province is, rather, the province of the heart: in its enclaves of farm and seaside village.

But it is no Elysium, no cure-all.

Here, starker than anywhere else, are the reminders of how inexorably one's address shifts from the letter to the tombstone; of what useless armour is the scarecrow, Thought, against the crows of Time.

To the already downhearted it is a land melancholy beyond description. Go there so lonely that each breath is another burning sup, deeper than pain, not from the air but from the airlessness inside you . . . and (both painter and sculptor of sentience incarnate) it will show you a statement of loneliness so far outmatching yours (though turned unreachably away from any link with it) that your breath will be nearly stripped from flesh by echoes of the unutterable:

A field of snow, dead of infinity before it fell, outdistancing its own eye as it stretches toward the gun-metal band of frozen light that bars all entrances to the horizon.

Beauty burning in each autumned leaf with the bladed light of all that's irrecoverable.

Unknown children, out of hearing, throwing a ball against the rain-eaten shingles of an unknown barn.

The last tree on the ridge of a slope down to the wanderer river.

A beam of moonlight striking the gilded fringe on the marker in the church Bible, open to Deuteronomy, and unseen from Sunday to Sunday.

A wild aster, a weed thinking it's a flower, blooming alone in the abandoned marsh.

A row of stakes leaning against the February dusk.

A face now but a shell of all its Junes.

A track.

A railway track.

A window tied the hours through to its own gaze by the wood that binds it in . . . .

But go there glad (and with another) and these very things change countenance. Attack no longer in them, they add the very bass notes (only apparently dissonant) that turn the simple octave of gladness into a deep-toned chord. Here too is where so much that seems like the stifled shriek of loneliness to an outsider is, to the native eye, through whatever storm or toil, merely the inmost and uttermost composure of things abiding by their own laws.

It is here too where *sounds* are still as pure and natural as the day that sound was born: harsh sometimes, but never Bedlamed like the steel-tongued sounds of cities and the war-worn noises in the clangoured streets:

The hum of furrows and the sound that Space makes in the sea.

The sound, honest as wheat, of the kindling catching fire in the kitchen stove, and the sound of brook water chuckling to itself just before you come in sight of it the first morning the sun says May.

Rain, not to bruise the darkness, falling straight down on the thirsting garden.

The resounding stillness inside a snowflake or a stone.

The one high amber note of the locust, straighter than lines and stabbing as regret, on the first September afternoon that smells of juniper.

The sound of the blacksmith's hammer on the anvil, its ringing clarity something almost visible in the air.

The clink of the cider mugs against the spigot when two neighbours, sweating together in the potato field, take fifteen minutes recess in the cellar cool as wells.

The sound of snowshoes on the woods trail, hardly louder than snowing; and the sound of bonfires, rustling as summer.

The sound of the pasture bars being lowered to give the cattle their first ecstatic taste of the springing timothy.

The adagio of the bedroom blind going up on a morning shimmering as truth.

The voices of man, wife, and children as they gather the spruce boughs to bank the house with, in a woods grove candider than noon.

The silence of plant cells growing, and of living growth healing its own wounds as nothing of man-shaped metal can.

The sound of silence inside the wheel and the sound of glory quiescent in the horse's nostril....

Nova Scotia is a place where so many inanimate things take on a living quality because of an intimacy nearly personal with the man amongst them. His grasp on the implement. His way of life hewn to the shifting seasons, as all that's chlorophylled is. Scarce anything around him but touches, in some way closer than the mere retinal, on his work and wonderment:

December axes and April harrows.

Leather traces with the surge of stallions never absent in them, and snow fences that hold against the gale.

September oats, golden in the sun (and golden to the touch too), and autumn mountains dressed for God.

Supper plates and weathervanes.

Graves and sugar maples.

Frost and stars....

Though in no way theatrical, here is where small plays are enacted in a few words or none at all.

"Dad, did you lift that great big rock up onto the stone wall?"

"No, my father did."

"Could you lift it?"

"No."

"Could anybody?"

"No."

"Were you scared of him?"

"No. Never."

A man is pruning his apple orchard: Kings, Russets, Bishop Pippins, and Wealthies.

In the crotch of a limb his saw strikes something hard. He draws the saw out before its teeth are ruined. He breaks the limb off with his own weight on it and splits it carefully with the axe.

The object the tree has grown over throughout the years falls out. A horseshoe. David, his first son, must have hung it there. He always hung up any horseshoe he found. For good luck.

For a moment he stands still—although he continues to breathe, and the bees forage as busily as ever in the breaking blossoms where the honey they live by is, and the mountains go on being mountains exactly as before.

If David had lived, he would be twenty-two now. They said David looked exactly like him, though they were not alike in any other way. David could multiply 22 by 1,987 in his head—and he could draw horses realer than horses. Where was all that now? Where, in what kind of twenty-two, was David now?

He sighs once, as a carpet of fallen leaves sighs (in the crucifictive light of October when someone you love has gone away forever) when a whitherless breeze leafs through it.

And then he takes the horseshoe to the house and finds a nail and a ladder and nails it as high as he can reach on the peak of the barn.

A man and his wife walk home from a funeral. They bend against the wind. The wind is from the North.

They pass the dead man's mailbox. Several letters of his name have been washed out by the fall rains.

"I remember when we was young," the man says, "Jim could run like a deer and swim like a fish. He could always hold his breath under water longer'n any of us. So long we'd start callin' to him. And I can see him cuttin' his initials into the bridge rail, while we stripped down and dived off it, with the pearl-handled jackknife he always kept sharp as a scythe."

"And do you remember," she says, "how that winter you had the broken wrist, he tended the cattle and saw to everything? I'll never forget it."

The kitchen is cold but the fire is laid. He touches the match (never needing more than one) to the twist of newspaper (telling of riots) beneath the chipyard splints and she puts fresh water into the teakettle.

"If you like that green dress in the catalogue," he says suddenly, "you send for it! We ain't paupers yet, and we're only goin' this way once."

A man's consciousness is shaped (consciously or not) by the trowel and drawknife of all that he has ever heard or seen or smelled or touched or tasted. More than that, by all that these sensations (sense-nations?) stand representatives of, all the nation of correlatives each brings (subconsciously) to mind.

Here, in Nova Scotia, is a richer composted infinity of such arousals (though none admixed with the character of any other) than almost anywhere else:

The frozen light of Genesis on the winter woodscape, and the fervent light of Luke on June's sparkling thistles.

Animals and animals' eyes.

Sunflowers and kingfishers.

The sound of the beef's skull when the sledge falls on it, and the hush of the fields when the hymns fall on them through the church window.

Jackdaws and Christmas spareribs.

Hemlock hills and seedling poppies.

The taste of head cheese, and the sight of the sky on the dusk when ghosts sit in all the crannies where hopes once sat.

Blizzards like madness, and the calm of the lake when it sleeps on its depth quieter than prayer books.

The green smell of the simple ground ivy, and the elliptical smell of the shape-proud plums.

Wildcats and dust devils.

The feel of your body when the hay lift invokes every muscle of it, and the feel of your body the morning (every blade of grass dancing with itself) your first son is born.

Lilacs and scarecrows.

The word "asunder" made shape in the ancient boulder the dynamite splits, and the intricate shirring on the underside of the mushroom that lives for one day . . . .

"Are you goin' in to town tonight to that big political meetin'?"

"Not damned likely! Them oily platform windbags? I never seen one o' them punkin-grinners yet I'd step across that *ditch* to shake hands with."

"Arth, could I borrow your spirit level? I'll take good care of it."

"Sure. Sure you can. How's the new house comin' on anyway?"

"Pretty fair. Soon as I make sure the crossbeam's level, I can start boardin' her in."

"That's when it'll do you good, man. It's like the first forenoon it's warm enough to take your coat off when you sow the barley. And we're damn glad you put the kitchen on the end this way. So's we can see your light."

A child brings home a piece of driftwood from the shore. The sea has scoured and antlered it the shape of care. He burns it in the open grate, to watch the coloured sparks.

"Why can't *water* burn?" he asks his mother.

"It wasn't made to," she says. "And, besides, all things are made so there's always one to stop another from having all its own way to do everything. The way water puts *out* fire."

For a moment she has a fearful vision of the ocean burning, and forgives it half her scars.

"Have you met the stranger that bought the old Marshall homestead?"

"No. But Tom Herald did."

"How did the new man strike him?"

"Tom said he liked him."

"That's good enough for me then. When it comes to judgin' people, I'd take that man ahead o' Solomon."

It is the kind of Christmas Eve when at four o'clock the snow begins to fall like no other snow in the year, kindling the whole air. More than Sundays know they are Sundays, the day knows it is the day before Christmas. It bathes everything with a kind of radiance less like glitter than a great unhiddenness. A great yielding of things and faces to each other.

A man walks down the mountain log road after the day's chopping. He is just tired enough for rest to give its most melodious soothing. Health is in him like a blush of safety. All questions have loosed their fish hooks from his brain.

No day could make less show of protective armament than this. But somehow its very tranquility mysteriously guards his heart as well from all those burning arrows of unfulfillment — when there is no one but the heart to hear the flinching of its own sighs (themselves a burning) for what is lost or can't be, for what is the more piercingly seen in the denial of it than it could ever be in the having.

He breathes deep of the clean Christmas-kindled air, and it seems as if there is spell enough of gentleness in it to purge the whole world of pain and wickedness.

From the edge of the clearing near the bottom of the mountain slope he has the first sight of his own lighted windows in the valley. As if the snow had caught its first sight of them too, the flakes begin less to eddy now than to fall straight down, giving the house over to the vivid care of the lights inside, and themselves (though in no separative way) to the cocooning of the darkening trees.

The man sees how it will be when he steps inside the house.

The spangling emerald tree, mild-mannered in the daytime as the snow, will now glint and jubilate and hallow without pause. And with the magic hush of peace that also comes from it (not as a silencer but as a seal on the shining) bring out the sudden speechfulness of everything here joined.

It will recruit even the casings and the doorways, scribes of the house, causing them for the length of Christmas to forget their memorizing and throw themselves in with the rest of the glowing present.

It will win the shadowed corners from their cornering and charm the parlour from its parlouring—until there is not a single space or face that is not totally one with every other.

He sees the supper table, splendid with the steam of Christmas food that is touched this night as if with miracle.

And, as if all wonders this night were brought close enough to be reached by the hand, he sees how the simple nearness of one face, his wife's, is more than all he'll ever need to keep his own face from crippling in the face of any day when the rain hangs sullen in the clouds that will not let it fall, or when the late November sun falls sadder than burials on the puddled swamp, or when the homeless winter winds blow the knuckles of the sky blue. . . .

He sees the eyes of his children, the boy's and the girl's, alive so swarmingly with what is now; and what will be, tomorrow.

And he sees (a miracle again) that of all the ways the children might have been, only in their being *exactly* this one, the way they are, could he have loved them anything like he does.

The blade of his discernment is brought to a finer edge by this fullness of heart than it could ever be brought to by any whetstone of suffering.

And as the snow falls thicker on the memoried road and as through the snow the lights mist softer as he nears them, he has a moment's surge of belonging ten times the measure of any longing's — when something other than thought or words tells him that his life is worth as much as any man's or king's, that the place where he lives and breathes in he would exchange for none on earth, and that he is happier than any man (or king) can be ....

An old woman is hooking a rug.

Age has drawn its final cancellation marks on her face. Not in the tragic lines of stricken beauty; but, more cruelly, to unshape its shapeliness into that mask of downfall flesh which makes a face nearly invisible (to any but children) once its eyes have lost their look of clasping.

Nowhere in the lying flesh can now be seen the days when her hair rang golden in the breeze, or the night when she danced the night through with the man with the handsomeness (she thought) like Christ's, who had just asked her to marry him.

But her hands are firm and steady, and somewhere inside her the directness of earlier days still burns as vividly as seventeen.

A mound of rags, torn into strips, lies beside her. Forgotten for years, these rags had lain in the attic, until she chanced on them today. Beneath the tray of oddments, forgotten too, in an old trunk. Some faded tintypes. A bundle of letters tied round with a tasselled string ("Dear Esther: I now take my pen in hand to let you know that we are well and hope you are the same. The weather is lovely today. I hope it lasts ..."). A bone-handled magnifying glass with the glass split down the middle ....

The kitchen steeps with calm as she draws the rags loop after loop through the canvas to a perfectly even height. The stove listens paternally to the kettle. The kettle hums to itself. The cat, all lassitude, the pouncing in its paws as if quite gone and unremembered, basks on the window sill the sun warms steadiest.

The afternoon is mid-June, when everything from leaf to cloud is gently bold with being its own utmost, and fearless as idols are of what comes next.

Sometimes when the year is young the woman feels the weight of her own years heaviest on her. But not today.

Today there is nothing her mind clutches at only to clutch nothingness. No sighing for the fled. No sense of feelings bruising themselves against the wall of what isn't. The gaze of the day is so open, as if denying troubles any place to *be*, that she herself feels (in the moments without thought) so peaceful, so un-opposite to anything, that her consciousness and what it sees become one and the same.

There is no pattern in her rug. No scrolls or flowers or imagery. There is a better way to use up these odds and ends she has today. Merely row after row of straight hooking, each row broken only by the varied lengths and colours of the rags that compose it.

It looks the simplest of rugs to make, but is by far the hardest to make well. A single ill-chosen length can botch it, or a single pair of misjoined colours.

She has the unhesitant gift of selection. So that, whenever her work is finished on a rug like this, there is a blaze, almost, of rightness about it. An unerringness such as she now sees in the sky or the trees or the garden (which she glances at sometimes for guidance or confirmation). There, where the extents of one colour and the one next it are so perfectly proportioned and the colours themselves always the two most perfectly conjoinable.

In the lulls the day allows her in its capture of her consciousness, she muses on the history of each strip of cloth she draws from the mound. From what garment did it come? By whom was it worn? By whom worn out?

This long strip of green (nearest green to the green of the second-grass the west-ering sun lacquers through the truth-bare bones of the chestnut trees as, alone, you rake the leaves beneath them in the chill unchilling air so clean that it lifts the heart with the glory of all that is assimilable and exquisitely stabs it with the challenge of what is not)—this she remembers. This was from the dress she'd made from the bolt of cloth the son who'd run away to sea brought her from the Hebrides when he brought his land-sick eyes back home.

She remembers that strip of yellow (the yellow nearest the distillate yellow, aching with purity, that the same sun transluminates the membranes of the parchment leaves with). That was (so long ago) from the lining of her dead child's cradle quilt: the first piece of silk ever to come into the house.

That strip of brown (nearest the burnish of the mahoganied chestnuts themselves) was from the laprobe she herself had spun and dyed for the double-seated sleigh.

She remembers that short strip of lavender. It was from a sash she had worn to the dances, when the dances were polkas and girls wore sashes.

That peacock blue—that was part of the scarf her husband wore as he skated on the frozen brook (and showed the children how) when grown men still skated their initials on the brook.

She remembers, from their remnants, this tablecloth (the neighbours had given it to them when they were first married) and those curtains, that bedspread and those valances: the things that ceaselessly talk their lives over in a house where three generations live happily together.

Those strips of plain grey (so like new) she can't recall. (They were from the "change of work shirt" her husband had ordered from the catalogue, but never worn—because just before it came, the change had suddenly been to the white shirt in the coffin. Somehow, because he had picked it out, she could never bring herself to send it back and get the money for it.)

But she remembers that poppy red. She sees the strips of real ribbon, their first extravagance, that went from the ceiling bell to the four corners of the parlour the first Christmas her husband had had money enough (from the keel pieces discovered on his timber lot) to surprise the children with presents that were not merely useful.

And that sapphire indigo. She sees the royal robe (of dyed blanket cloth) that her first grandson wore the night he was the Wise Man (aged ten) who bore the "frankincense" (in a tureen she had silvered over with tea lead) in the school play's Nativity scene.

And that white white. Yes, those were all the strips of lace she used to crochet for "inserts" in all her Sunday dresses, when women wore lace....

Turning the mound over, she picks up a strip of imitation velvet (from a shawl a cousin in the city had once sent her) and hooks it in. She sees it is wrong. She ravels it back.

Her great-grandson comes into the kitchen and sits down beside her. He is seven, and he has the child of seven's moteless gaze.

"Gram," he says, "what makes so many cracks in your face?"

"Cracks?"

"Yes. There's *more* . . . when you laugh like that."

"Yes," she says, "they can come from laughing. I did laugh a lot. And I suppose I got some from the day the colt your grandfather was breaking to the wagon ran away and plunged into the railway cut, right in front of the train. The train broke its neck, and nearly his. And some, I suppose, from the day the forest fires were so thick and close around the houses the grass was burning too and we took the children and stood in the brook with them until some miracle sent the rain. And...."

"Do you get them from being married?"

"Yes. But they're the best kind. The worst kind's the kind you get when you've got nothing to trouble you. Not a chick nor a child. When there's no one you can say, 'What would *you* do?' to, when trouble comes."

"Will I get them someday?"

"Yes, child. Everybody does. But don't you worry. You won't shrivel up like that. You'll have things happen to you, I can see. You're like your grandfather. You'll make them happen. You'll have the best kind of wrinkles in your face."

"I didn't mean I didn't like your face, Gram."

"I know."

"When we've got something special for supper, like trout, you slip some offa your plate onto mine, don't you."

"Sometimes."

"And when I want to do something they can't see why I want to do it, you know why, the very first one, don't you."

"Sometimes."

"I didn't mean I didn't like your face, Gram."

"I know, child, I know."

"You laughed, didn't you? We can always make each other laugh, can't we?"

He sorts through the mound of rags and passes her another strip of brown (it is from the earth-brown Prince Albert coat of his grandfather). She sees that the colour is just right. She hooks it in.

"Gram," he says, "when you get old, do you know everything?"

"No," she says. "Only a few things. You know that a wild strawberry blossom is as much as a mountain. You know that a face is more than all the mountains, or the rivers. You know that 'yes' is more than 'no' ...."

"Sometimes you talk funny," he says, grinning, "but it's not . . . funny talk. Sometimes I don't know what you mean, but I know . . . what you *mean*."

It is a curious thing about the human being that he so often feels he owes Life (or *some*thing) his measure of sadness. If he tries to blur the pain by any activity that crowds it out, he somehow feels that he is shirking a duty.

Least of all are Nova Scotians like this. They don't sup jealously on their own sorrows.

Not quite Stoics (they're too funded with feeling for that), neither are they like the mediaeval larks that sang the braver for having their eyes put out. They see things clearer than metaphysicians, though any loftiness of speech they spurn or laugh out of countenance. They bend to life's prime hardships as they come, but bow to nothing. Not to December's fierce temper. Not to August's fierce heat. Not to the shriek of absences. Not to plans turned ash. Not to the death of family or friends. Not to their own death itself.

They are not giants or heroes in any way (they'd laugh if you told them they were) — but their essences are richer than most. And what any account of them must recurrently come back to is the constant interplay of their senses with what is everlastingly intrinsic and near; until finally they come as if to have a common bloodstream with it. A current that puts them in the presence, at least, of all the vastnesses of implication in each particle (each a universe) that surrounds them. This, if not in their head, is in their bones, in instance after instance.

The crowing of the rooster is thus shorthand for all the trumpets of Morning.

The blackening of the night-struck brook is all sorcery.

The smell of the auger shavings all willingness.

The clench of ice upon itself all strength.

The clench of rocks upon themselves all fortitude.

The touch of firewood the key to satisfaction.

The taste of ruby-red beet wine all expectation.

The fern-shaped patterns the frost draws with its diamond on the moonlit pane all grace.

The chaliced lichen on the stone all courage.

Some snows, the way they lie, hinting all gain.

Some snows, the way they lie, all loss.

Some hills all Easters, some hills all judgments.

Whatever flaw is just missing in the perfect flower paradoxically all love.

Some sundowns (striking their endless and perfect sets from second to second) all hope; some all defeat.

Shadows that can't be held, distances of field that yield no answer to the heart's vain questions, shores that watch the gulls fly out of sight — all yearning.

Heads of ripened wheat (and wild cherry blossoms that extol the air) all joy.

The funeral hush in the spokes of the motionless wheel that the snow sifts through saying more about Death than the dead.

The spiral marking on the snail's snug house infinity. . . .

Yes, again and again such correspondences as these—as many hundreds of them as a man has feelings different from each other in kind or degree.

And with them, again and again, countless to a day, all those unindexable tangents of import behind the simplest fact, which populate and parable even the scantiest spirit.

And beside *them,* again and again, yet another multitude without end: the objects (not object lessons) that are merely the bare nouns of themselves, but so stipple the Nova Scotian's inner weather with the awareness and imprint of how many *kinds* of thing there *are* that he is never trapped in that terrible echo chamber of monotony, where incessantly what you breathe in is what you breathe out is what you breathe in again. . . .

Storm door latches patinaed by how many hands and philosophied by how many weathers.

Paths between one house and another, their pathness a more neighbourly thing for its never being straight.

Fence posts stripped to everything but perpendicularity as each looks blindly away from the next in line, all snowscapes long, toward the family trees in the hackmatack grove they came from.

Mailboxes but a dozen swaths of grass away from headstones.

Grindstones not quite an eye-swath away from the transcendent white church spire.

Thorns and water lilies.

Fox dens and flying squirrels.

Barn shadows hypotenused stricter than algebra on the dawning field, and blueberry blossoms in the shape of bells.

The hands of your wife as they rub in the soothing liniment between your shoulder blades where they suffered the sprain (as nearly happily remembered now as the sprain of love) when you held back the rolling force-blind log from crushing your fellow worker on the capsized load.

All the hands that bear witness to the bed-rock things they've handled for their living, and configure all the history of their living's days that even the supremely archival eyes leave out.

The touch of the girl child's hair, all innocence, before it too learns the wiliness of the world's coin.

The gust of the boy child's semblance to you when you pass him (conscience forbidding) the terrible electricity of the gun.

The gun itself, a companion close as suicide in the crook of your arm, as you walk purified of trivia in the hunt of the haunted woods . . . and suddenly (conscience forgotten) search for the heart of the deer within the savage dusk.

The sap (sometimes as if totally your own) of the maples, and the salt (always tantalizingly not quite yours) of the sea.

The grandchild's face sleeping against the grandfather's knee . . . and the vanished face, bleaching your own, returned again to put the fieldness back into the fields, the houseness back into the house, the skyness back into the sky, the roadness back into the road, the is-ness back into everything there is. . . .

Nova Scotia is no Shangri-La. As far from that as trials from their answers.

Blunter sometimes than handspikes, bleaker sometimes than trust betrayed or epiphanies too late, it is that often more locust for the heart than lotus. Its exclamations can be redundant. Its rigours are knuckled as stubbornness. Its beauties are not always without the lectern sternness of their own immaculacy, which is like a dare behind them to absorb what they manifest in all its fullness if you can.

(Though the dare softens when the eye confesses its weakness.) Some days it can be as tender as an Indian embracing his hostless, countryless, dream-faced child at the elevation of the Host; others, as brutal as goodbye or indifferent as perhaps.

Yet it is Gibraltarly (though not haughtily) valid; and, like few other places, always recognizes that you *too* are there.

At a glance, it is repetitious. Its main constants are not many. But as one snow or one loneliness is totally different from another, or as a face you love is many-ed according as the play of expression transforms it from thought to thought, so is each of these constants thousandly different according as the "lighting" on it, or its context, is thousandly different. (How immense the diversity within its Hiroshimas of sunset or its Hallelujahs of bloom or its green shade when set against the green shade on the light bulb the man works under who follows the ticker tape or decodes the stutter of telegrams!)

Nova Scotia is a supreme linguist and interpreter. And here is where a man can learn what excitement it is to *watch* the nebulous made creature, the translation of his every smoke-shaped feeling (with all its Moorish shadows) into solid guise.

A land as exhaustively detailed as this is like a person. And so, like a person, unencompassable by any nets of words the tongue throws out. Neither by any mode of dissection or addition. (Can you find the music by taking the piano apart? How can you add together the child's hands clasped together in his lap, having so soon learned the comfort in each other, and the old man's failure to split the knotted beech, as he once did, with a single blow of the axe?) Yet here is no scattering of blind particulars, but a living organism.

Nova Scotia has no linear equalities within itself, but (taking the sea as base) it forms an isosceles triangle with the man who loves it; welding him, where their equal sides converge, to the universals. And though itself the least given to hyperbole, of nowhere can it be said with more truth that here is where the heart meets its match in every sense of the word.

Counterfeit and Coin

The handwriting is on the well—and on the dory. The spirit of *this* Nova Scotia seems to be fast disappearing to wherever the spirit of a countryside flees when others than the planters put their brass and specious touch on it. Whether (opinions differ) an occasion for hurrah or alas—"progress," the advance spy of Babel and steel, has already begun to infiltrate and infest the land, begun to shoulder its individuality aside and mark it out for parcelment.

Already in some districts the box-eyed houses, some of them with box-eyed occupants, are trying to make conformity regnant; trying to tame by imprisonment in the dismal plots of their backyards the grass that was once (with the trees) king of the whole landscape. The land is beginning to smother beneath all the crockery of man that is being heaped on it.

Brick stares where wood used to smile. Bulldozers disrespect stones that men were once proud to lift. Shopping Centres (with their aisles of marked-down goods putting as if an ash on the quick of the crowd-drubbed faces of the people who wander them) spring up where once were orchards. Television aerials comb the night for dross or screams where once the night kissed righteous muscles with the balm of rest. Faces in the bus, travelling like luggage (while the air brakes unconsciously shunt their breath more dreadfully than a sigh of Christ's, and the skimmed-eyed waitresses at the midway restaurant brace the counter with stoups of caffeine and cruets of vinegar for the daily gut of loneliness), scan each other's locks where faces once were joined by glances as if by hyphens of light. Doubts lean where certainties once stood. . . .

And yet. And yet in other districts there are still things like these:

Kingfishers still circle the meadows. Pebbles pure-white as the first particle that knew it was silver jewel the beds of innocent brooks. Gods of primal force, like Thors and Odins to the man's own trifling strength, both awe and exhilarate him as they ride the chain lightning or walk on the shoulders of mountains beneath the frost-glint of stars. A man carries his son home on his shoulders after a long day's mission blazing lines in the holy forest. Neighbours enact their substantive noun when there's a neighbour's sickness in the night; as friends do theirs, the cindered and the green times through. Children laugh without being told what's funny. Un-citied weathers still find an untouched place to be themselves. Partridges, alert as trigonometry, still feed on the crimson seed sacs of the wild roses, and ferns the height of deer still ennoble the air around them like Plantagenets the field of honour. Some houses are still chroniclers, some hills still revelations — it is in these places that it can be seen how Nova Scotians own the sighting of their own eyes as few men do.

The born Nova Scotian owns his own name and answers to it without hesitation at the challenge of whatever roll call. He owns his own blood. And his is the most remembering of all bloods. The tincture of heritage from that of his forbears is always constitutively in him in the miraculous way that a single tear is said to tincture, with its disinfectant, seas of water; in the way that a man's resemblance to his great-grandparent across the forehead is transmitted in a pinpoint of sperm. Even now, the gait of original freedom stubbornly in him and his fellows, he never has to go far to find another Nova Scotian with a like spine: to match itself against annihilation by the juggernaut which levels all things to sameness. Enough of these men may yet stop it dead in its tracks. Their spirit may yet prevail, as the simplest green plant can split the clench of stone and break out its green leaves above it.

Faith (and where else can faith for the future be placed?) must look too to the young. Here as elsewhere they are often labelled slovenly, rootless, nothing but destructive . . . all that. But the best of them (who are by far the greater majority) have seen through the trinkets of material success, have (with their acute ear) heard the rattle of dry bones in the sepulchral vaults where "familiars" of the megamachine reside, and are not prepared to buy with their lives the fat and fictions of the plush-lined occupation. In growing numbers they are searching for work that will fulfill not the pocket but the exercise of what a man among men is. Or should be. Not many will go back to the plough, for sure; and yet their stand is not too implausible an echo of the ploughman's whose touchstone is the candid and the candid only.

With these assorted armies to defend it, the essential Nova Scotia may yet survive. Or may not.

But one thing is certain. As long as one wild hawthorn breaks dauntless through the wilderness of chrome or a single dogwood bravely blossoms, its history will be kept. And come what may, the sea beside it (that the rains of Spring and the snows of Winter equally melt into) will never lose its fierce dominion.

"Dad, did you lift that great big rock up onto the stone wall?"

"No, my father did."

"Could you lift it?"

"No."

"Could anybody?"

"No."

"Were you scared of him?"

"No. Never."